Timeless Child

Pen & Pencil Play - Into the Zone

Mandala Magnificence

Designed by Toni the Doodler

DEDICATION

I dedicate this to all the colourists/colorists that I am very much enjoying getting to know.

ACKNOWLEDGMENTS

There are a few people who no matter what, continue to encourage me to keep going, you know who you are. As a result of their continued encouragement, I am happy to release the second of my 'Into the Zone' series of colouring books and I've been gently beavering away in my own little zone, feeling the most contented that I ever have because I'm doing what I'm meant to. I have also do animal portraits, thanks to the unfaltering enthusiasm and encouraging anticipation of a wonderful friend who's faith in me leaves me humble and grateful.

Thank you Gareth.

In this second volume I have created a variety of mandalas; not hand drawn this time as I know some of you prefer the accuracy of computer designed pieces. I love the infinite variations that you can get and I find that even the creation of these fascinating designs is very relaxing in itself, not to mention the fun of coloring them. I've tried to provide mandalas of different levels of complexity (though I personally find it quite challenging to make simple designs as it's so much fun playing with them and seeing what I can do next. Please let me know what you liked most and least and an idea of the reasons why. And, as before, please post up your finished pieces on my Facebook page.

Find Toni The Doodler on Facebook:
https://www.facebook.com/Toni.the.Doodler/

And her website is:
http://timelesschildarts.wix.com/toni-the-doodler

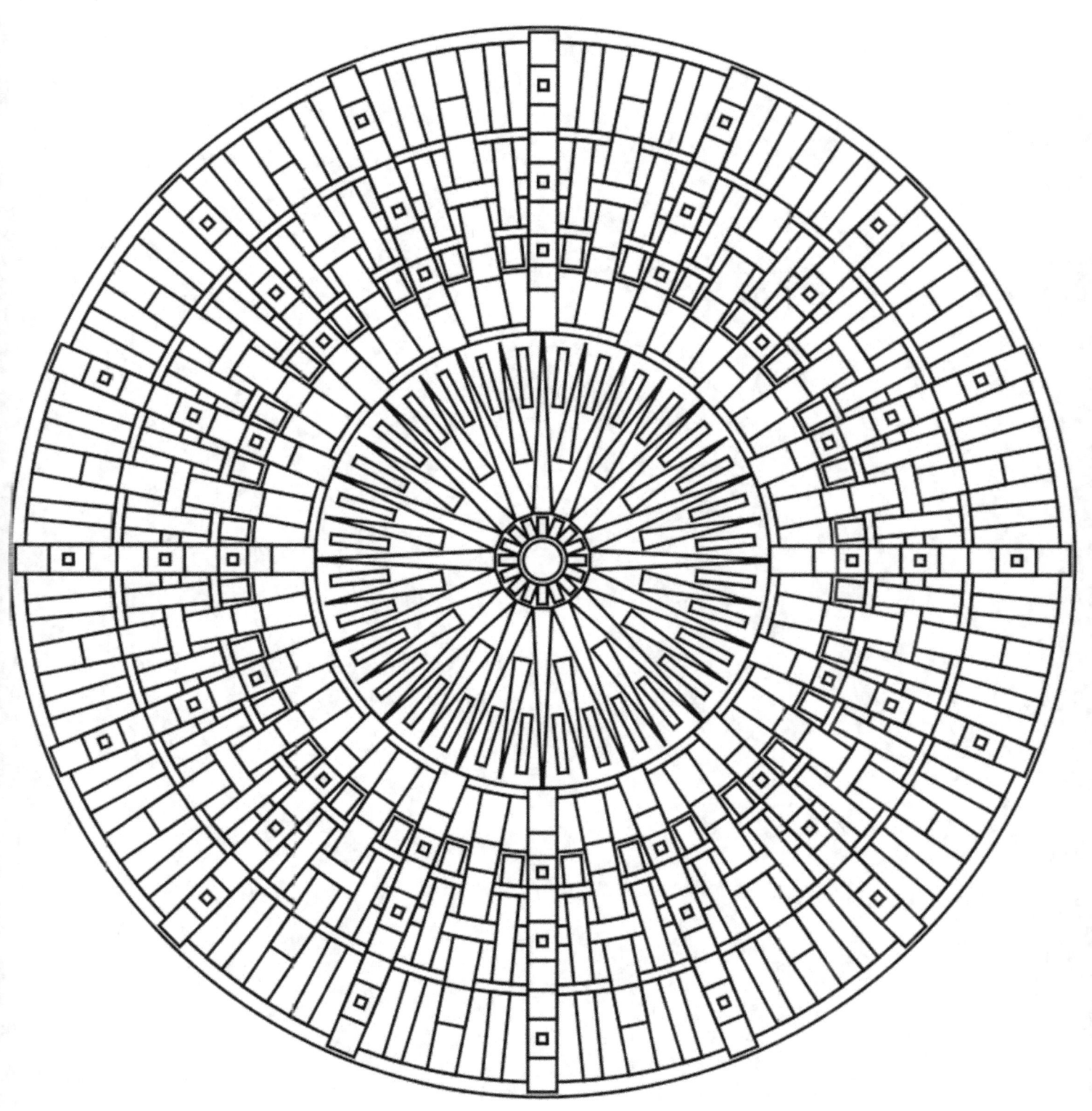

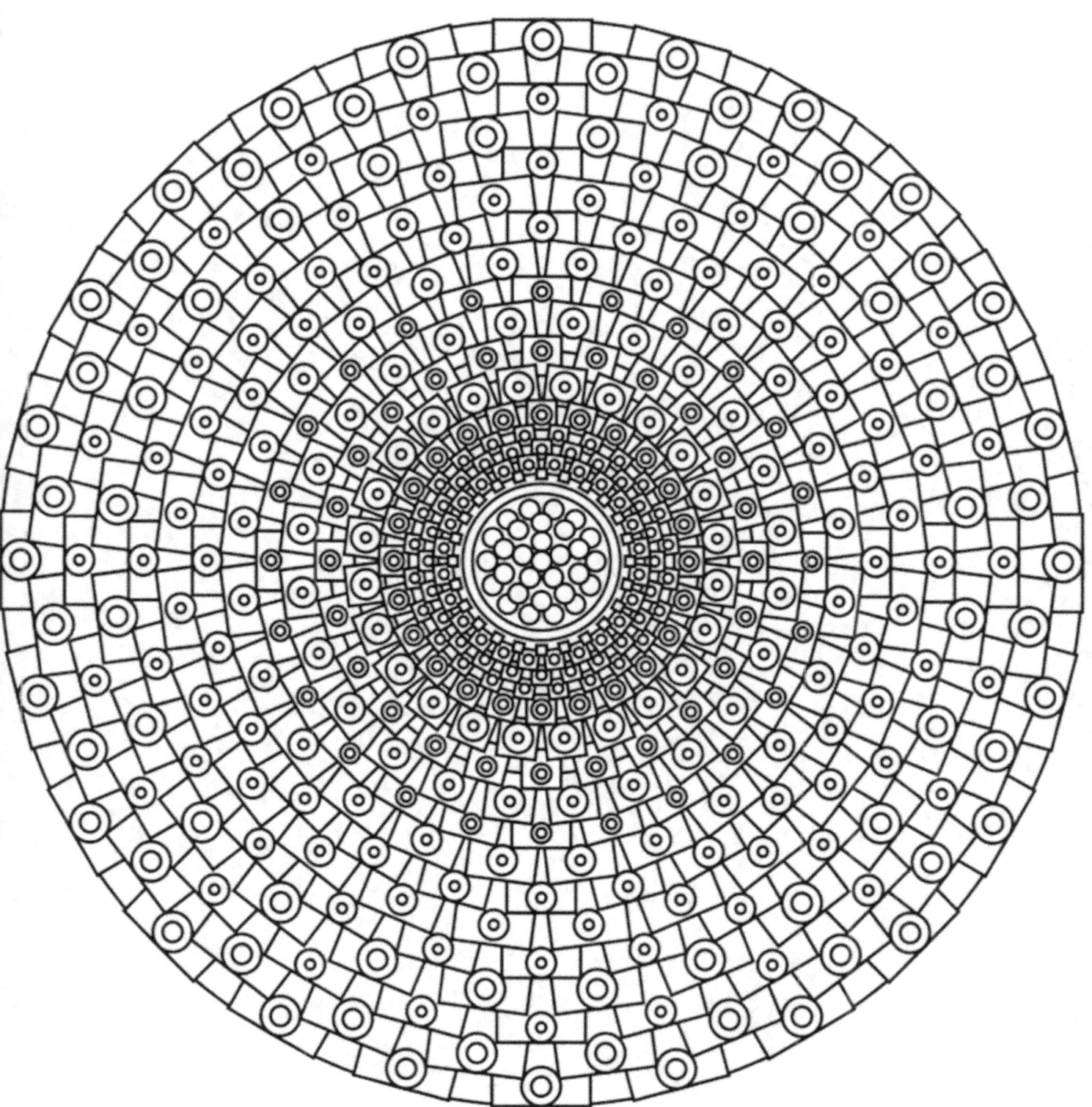

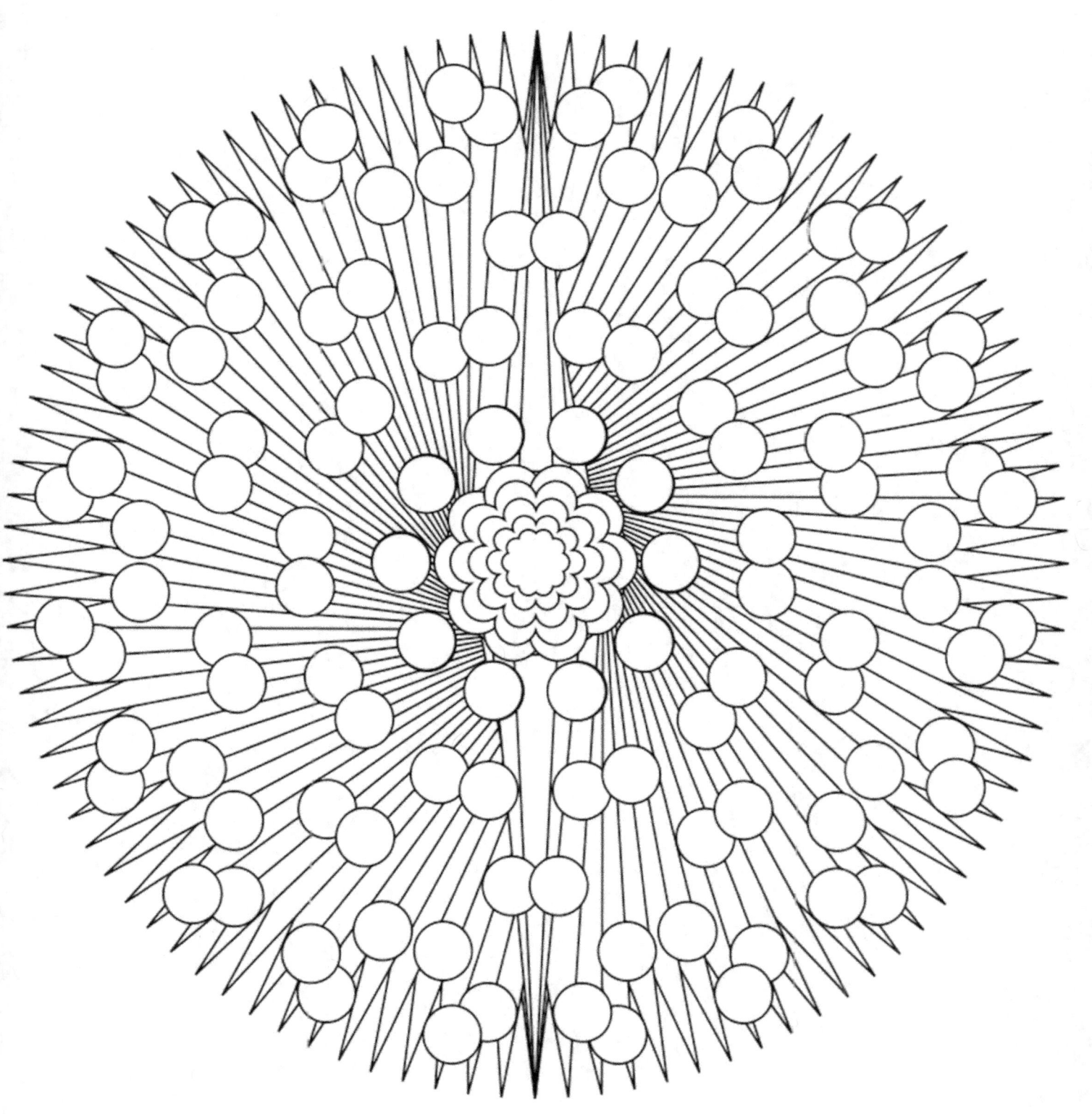

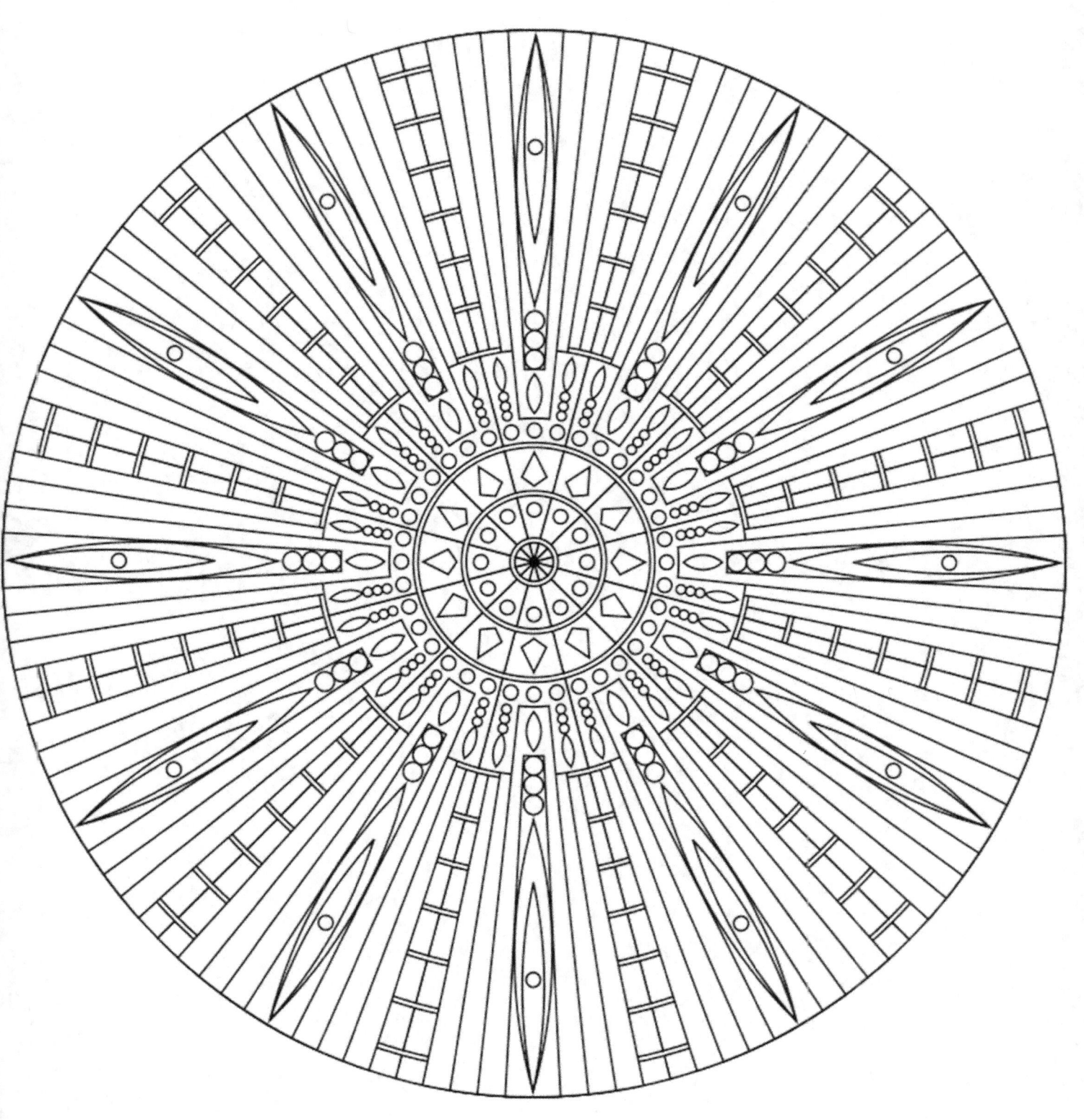

Timeless Child is the brand name of the works completed by Toni the Doodler. Toni was born in London in 1963 and is an artist and a poet, with lengthy interruptions to her creative existence while doing 'proper jobs' as advised by her 'elders and betters'. Now returning to art in its many forms, she feels closer to being herself when creating her artwork from painting and drawing (pet portraits a speciality) through colouring books to glass painting and poetry which ranges anywhere from greetings, through passionate and loving, to dark and disturbed. She creates colouring books and plans a series of volumes of her poetry.

Based in the UK, Toni has four adult children, 2 boys and 2 girls, sharing her home with her youngest son and their dog who can generally be found by her side.

Find her on Facebook and upload your coloured pages:
http://www.facebook.com/Toni.the.Doodler/

Her website is:
http://timelesschildarts.wix.com/Toni-the-Doodler

www.ingramcontent.com/pod-product-compliance
Lightning Source LLC
Chambersburg PA
CBHW081554280526
45788CB00011B/3466